# Financial Statement Analysis: The Blueprint For Investing Success

Andrew P.C.

Copyright © 2017 Andrew P.C.

All Rights Reserved

D1737567

# Contents

# <u>About The Author</u>

Hi, I'm Andrew.

Ever since college, I became fascinated with investing. I even got my degree in accounting and finance!

There's just something amazing about having your money work for you! After college, I got my first real job as an equity research analyst (just a fancy term for someone who researches stocks).

Since then, I've been lucky enough to be exposed to many different aspects of investing. Most people I come across are scared of investing. But it's a necessary skill to learn in order to prepare for retirement.

That's why it is my goal to teach more people about the benefits of investing!

Check out my website, www.DividendGrowthMasters.com to get more great (and free) content!

Also, check out the back of this book for an amazing deal

on my online financial statement analysis course! I will personally teach you how to invest!

**PLUS for being loyal readers, I'll be giving away FREE BONUS CONTENT with the course worth over $160!**

Financial Statement Analysis is the backbone of successful investing.

The best investors of all time (think Warren Buffett, David Einhorn, Jim Chanos, etc.) all read SEC filings on a daily basis. The truth is most investors never even crack open a 10-K or 10-Q or even bother reading a Proxy statement.

**If you read these SEC filings on a regular basis, you can get a real competitive edge on other investors.**

Don't worry, if you've passed fourth grade English you can definitely read a financial statement. More often than not, teachers over-complicate the subject by using fancy terms or poor examples.

The purpose of this book is to teach you how to read financial statements and SEC filings to get a real investing advantage.

I first began reading financial statements in my sophomore year in college. After I graduated, I took a job as an equity research analyst. Since then, I've studied hundreds of companies and have read thousands of filings.

You'll get a real insider's look on how to read financial statements to improve your investing success rate. Everything you learn here will be applicable right away.

**By the end of this book, you'll be able to:**

*Calculate and interpret important financial ratios

*Evaluate leverage

*Understand key valuation methodologies

*Read key SEC filings

*Understand key performance indicators in a variety of industries

*Dig up key information to get a competitive edge against other investors.

Thank you for reading and I hope this book is helpful!

# Financial Statement Overview

Financial statements convey the results and financial position of a business. They are the primary output used to evaluate a company's business prospects, sales, profitability, cash flow, and various other metrics.

In the U.S., financial statements are prepared on a quarterly and annual basis. In certain parts of Europe and other international countries, financial statements are only reported on a semi-annual basis.

**There are four types of financial statements:** (1) the income statement, (2) the balance sheet, (3) the statement of cash flows, and (4) the statement of stockholder's equity.

The statement of stockholder's equity isn't used too frequently in financial statement analysis so it will not be a big focus in this book.

## The Balance Sheet

The purpose of the balances sheet is to give investors an idea of (1) what assets the company owns, (2) what it owes to creditors (i.e. debt), and (3) the capital invested (and re-invested) by shareholders. In other words, the balance sheet displays all of the company's assets, liabilities, and equity at a point in time.

<u>Assets represent things that provide future economic benefits to a company.</u>

An example of an asset would be an office building, which provides space for the company to conduct business activities. It could also be a patent, which provides intellectual property protection for inventions. An asset can even be merchandise inventory, which can be sold for a profit.

Liabilities are the direct opposite of assets. <u>Liabilities represent the company's future economic sacrifices.</u>

If the company has a loan outstanding from the bank, the future economic sacrifice is (1) the payment of periodic interest and (2) the repayment of the loan's principal balance. If the company has accounts payable due to supply vendors, the future economic sacrifice is paying the vendor.

<u>Equity represents the capital (i.e. cash) shareholders have</u>

invested in the company plus cumulative profits that have been retained/re-invested in the business.

Let's discuss the presentation of the balance sheet. **The assets and liabilities on the balance sheet are often split into current and non-current classifications** as shown below in Costco's most recent balance sheet:

*The assets portion of Costco's balance sheet*

| | August 28, 2016 | | August 30, 2015 |
|---|---|---|---|
| **ASSETS** | | | |
| **CURRENT ASSETS** | | | |
| Cash and cash equivalents | $ 3,379 | $ | 4,801 |
| Short-term investments | 1,350 | | 1,618 |
| Receivables, net | 1,252 | | 1,224 |
| Merchandise inventories | 8,969 | | 8,908 |
| Other current assets | 268 | | 228 |
| Total current assets | 15,218 | | 16,779 |
| **PROPERTY AND EQUIPMENT** | | | |
| Land | 5,395 | | 4,961 |
| Buildings and improvements | 13,994 | | 12,618 |
| Equipment and fixtures | 6,077 | | 5,274 |
| Construction in progress | 701 | | 811 |
| | 26,167 | | 23,664 |
| Less accumulated depreciation and amortization | (9,124) | | (8,263) |
| Net property and equipment | 17,043 | | 15,401 |
| **OTHER ASSETS** | 902 | | 837 |
| **TOTAL ASSETS** | $ 33,163 | $ | 33,017 |

*The liabilities section of Costco's balance sheet*

| LIABILITIES AND EQUITY | | | | |
| --- | --- | --- | --- | --- |
| CURRENT LIABILITIES | | | | |
| Accounts payable | $ | 7,612 | $ | 9,011 |
| Current portion of long-term debt | | 1,100 | | 1,283 |
| Accrued salaries and benefits | | 2,629 | | 2,468 |
| Accrued member rewards | | 869 | | 813 |
| Deferred membership fees | | 1,362 | | 1,269 |
| Other current liabilities | | 2,003 | | 1,695 |
| Total current liabilities | | 15,575 | | 16,539 |
| LONG-TERM DEBT, excluding current portion | | 4,061 | | 4,852 |
| OTHER LIABILITIES | | 1,195 | | 783 |
| Total liabilities | | 20,831 | | 22,174 |

**Current assets and liabilities are those that will be consumed, paid off, or settled within the next year.** Examples include accounts receivable due from customers, merchandise inventory, or accounts payable due to suppliers.

**In contrast, non-current assets and liabilities are those that will not be consumed, paid off, or settled within the next year.** These are the long-term assets and liabilities of the business. Examples include factory production equipment, office real estate, and long-term bank obligations.

The reason for the current and non-current classification is to give investors a better understanding about the short-term and long-term liquidity needs of the business.

The balance sheet is an essential tool for investors because it shows all of the Company's assets and liabilities. **The balance sheet is a great tool to quickly evaluate the**

**financial health of the business.** Obviously, we would not be interested in investing in a business saddled with insurmountable debt.

In later chapters, we'll go through a few ways to evaluate the quality of a balance sheet.

☐

## The Income statement

**The income statement summarizes a company's profit generating activities--meaning its revenues and expenses.**

The income statement shows revenues and expenses over a period of time. For instance, an annual income statement shows the company's revenues and expenses from the beginning of the year until the end of the year.

Most companies prepare something called a **multi-step income statement.** This just means there are various subtotals for profit accounts throughout the statement.

Let's look at an example first. This what an income statement will look like for many companies:

| JC. Co. Income Statement For The Year Ended 12/31/16 | |
|---|---|
| Revenue | $100,000 |
| Cost of goods sold | ($50,000) |
| **Gross Profit** | **$50,000** |
| Operating expenses: | |
| Selling expenses | ($10,000) |
| General and administrative | ($10,000) |
| Research & development | ($5,000) |
| **Operating Income** | **$25,000** |
| Other income (expense) | |
| Interest income | $500 |
| Interest expense | ($500) |
| **Income before taxes** | **$25,000** |
| Income tax expense | ($10,000) |
| **Net income** | **$15,000** |

**Revenue** (also known as sales) is the top line item of any company's income statement. Revenue simply represents the sale of goods/services to customers.

If a company generates revenue from several different sources (i.e. service vs. products), it may decide to disclose them separately.

Below the revenue line is **cost of inventory** also known as cost of goods sold (COGS). **Cost of goods sold** represents the cost paid to acquire/produce inventory for sale. For Costco, it would represent the cost to purchase inventory at wholesale prices.

Services companies may not have any cost of goods sold. Instead, they'll have "cost of services", which may include expenses such as employee salaries required to provide the service.

**Gross profit** represents the difference between revenue and cost of goods sold/cost of services.

Below the gross profit line is all of the company's other operating expenses. These operating expenses are needed to run the day to day operations.

These operating expenses include:

*****Selling expenses**: These are expenses incurred to generate sales such as marketing, advertising, and sales commissions.

*****General and administrative expense**: These are back office expenses that support the business such as costs related to accounting and financial reporting, call center operations, etc.

**\*Research and development expenses (R&D):** These are common expenses in the technology and pharmaceutical industry. These are expenses incurred to develop new products.

**Operating income/profit** is left after subtracting all operating expenses from gross profit. This is the core income of the business.

Below the operating income line item are various **other income and expense items.** These are miscellaneous items such as interest income on cash in the bank or interest expense on debt outstanding. It may even include gains or losses from asset sales.

**Income before taxes** is what is left after subtracting other income/expenses from operating income.

Finally, **net income** represents income before taxes less taxes. Net income is the take home profit from the business after deducting all expenses.

**The Statement of Cash Flows**

**<u>The statement of cash flows shows how a company's cash</u>**

**balance changed over time.** This is an important financial statement to focus on because it shows the inflows and outflows of cash.

The statement of cash flows classifies cash transactions into three categories: (1) operating activities, (2) investing activities, and (3) financing activities.

**Cash from operating activities** represents cash inflows and outflows from a company's main business activities. This involves changes in a company's working capital. By working capital, I mean current assets and current liabilities. Remember, these are assets and liabilities that will be consumed within one year.

Examples of cash inflows from operating activities include cash received from the sale of goods and services to customers, interest income on cash investments, and dividends from investments.

Examples of outflows include purchases of inventory, employee wages, office building rent, various operating expenses, interest on debt, and of course, income taxes.

**Cash from investing activities** refers to inflows and outflows related to the purchase or sale of non-current assets. Remember, non-current assets refers to assets that provide benefits for more than one year.

Examples of cash from investing activity items include the purchase or sale of office buildings, investments in stocks/bonds, and acquisitions (or divestitures) of businesses.

The final section of the statement of cash flows is cash from financing activities. **Financing activities** relate to the external financing of the company. In other words, any transactions related to debt or equity financing.

Inflows from financing activities include selling shares to stockholders or borrowing money from the bank.

Cash outflows include dividends paid to shareholders, repurchases of shares from shareholders, or repayment of the principal balance of debt.

The reason for the cash flow statement classifications is to better understand how a business is using its cash. We want to know how much it is generating from core operations, how much it is investing in long-term assets, and how much external financing is required to keep the business running.

**If we just combined all three sections into one long statement, it would be difficult to judge the cash flow generation capability of the business.**

## Earnings-Per-Share (EPS)

Shares represent units of ownership in a business that typically provide for an equal distribution of profits and dividends.

All pubic companies have freely tradeable shares. This means that they are traded on stock exchanges as opposed to private companies whose shares are privately traded.

Each share in a public company typically gives the holder one vote in shareholder matters.

There are two different ways to express share count (the number of shares a company has outstanding)

**Basic shares outstanding** represents the number of shares outstanding.

However, shares are not the only way for stockholders to hold ownership interests in a business. Companies frequently issue stock options, restricted stock, and other equity awards to compensate executives.

These equity awards represent the right to receive shares and act as share dilution to current stockholders.

**Diluted share count** is a more conservative approach to calculate the number of shares outstanding. Diluted shares outstanding represents basic shares outstanding plus any other potential claims on common shares.

Let's say a company has 200 shares outstanding from raising capital to start operations. At the end of the year, the company decides to compensate the CEO with 10 stock options, with each option allowing the CEO to acquire one share.

In this example, basic shares outstanding would be 200 shares and the diluted share count would be 200 + 10 or 210 shares.

The most common way to utilize share count in financial analysis is to express a company's earnings on a per-share basis. This is referred to earnings-per-share or EPS. **EPS** represents the amount of profit the company generates for every share outstanding.

**An EPS of $2.00 means the company generates two dollars for**

**every share outstanding.**

There are two ways to express EPS: basic and diluted EPS.

**Basic EPS** represents net income divided by basic shares outstanding.

**Diluted EPS** represents net income divided by diluted shares outstanding.

Diluted EPS is the more commonly used metric in financial analysis because it provides a more conservative calculation than basic EPS.

**Profitability Metrics**

The most common profitability metrics used in financial analysis include: (1) gross margin, (2) operating margin, and (3) net margin.

Profitability ratios are widely used to assess how much profit a business brings in for every dollar of sales generated. Obviously, it is more advantageous to have a higher margin.

**Gross margin** is calculated as gross profit divided by revenue expressed as a percentage.

$$\text{Gross Margin} = \frac{\text{Gross Profit}}{\text{Revenue}}$$

Remember, gross profit represents revenue less cost of goods sold. Gross margin represents the amount of gross profit the company generates per dollar of revenue.

A gross margin of 50% that means for every dollar of revenue, the Company generates 50 cents of gross profit.

Gross margin is a widely used metric because it measures the cost of delivering a product or service to a customer. Higher gross margins are typically associated with businesses that have high barriers to entry.

Conversely, lower gross margins are more often associated with businesses that have lower barriers to entry (like restaurants or retail stores).

<u>When comparing gross margin, it is important to remember different industries will have entirely different margin profiles.</u> For example, software companies typically have very high gross margins (i.e. 80-90%+) relative to retail businesses (60% or lower).

**Operating margin** represents operating income over revenue expressed as a percentage. Remember, operating income is gross profit less operating expenses.

$$\text{Operating Margin} = \frac{\text{Operating Profit}}{\text{Revenue}}$$

Operating margin represents the amount of operating income generated per dollar of sales. An operating margin of 20% means for every dollar of sales, the Company generates 20 cents of operating profit.

Finally, net margin is calculated net income divided by revenue expressed as a percentage. Net income represents revenue less all expenses (including taxes).

Net margin describes how much profit the business takes home per dollar of revenue generated. A net profit margin of 15%, means the business makes 15 cents per dollar of revenue generated.

$$\text{Net Margin} = \frac{\text{Net Income}}{\text{Revenue}}$$

Typically, analysts compare profitability metrics relative to (1) prior year results or (2) some peer or competitor in the same industry.

The reason to compare margins to prior year results is to get an understanding of how profitability has changed. If margins are down is it because of higher input prices, lower selling prices, and/or increased competition?

The reason to compare margins relative to peers and competitors is to get a better understanding of how the company has performed on a relative basis. If the company's margins are below peers is it because of inefficient manufacturing? Poor marketing?

Conversely, if margins are above peers is it because of better scale? Or maybe because of cost synergies? Those are kind of thoughts to consider when comparing margins relative to peers.

The way we compare percentages in finance is through basis points (bps). **A basis point represents 1/100th of a percent.**

.01% represents 1 basis point.

1% represents 100 basis points.

☐

**Analyzing Activity And Turnover Ratios**

Activity/turnover ratios are very important financial metrics because they gauge the ability to convert assets into cash.

Let's look at asset turnover first. **Asset turnover** is calculated as sales divided by average total assets. Average assets simply means the balance of assets between the beginning and end of the period.

$$\text{Asset Turnover:} \quad \frac{\text{Sales}}{\text{Average Assets}}$$

Asset turnover depicts how efficiently a business uses its assets to generate sales.

For instance, an asset turnover ratio of 1.2 means that the business generates 1.2 dollars in sales per dollar invested in assets. Obviously, a higher asset turnover is more desirable.

**Accounts Receivable Turnover**

Most business transactions are not conducted with cash, but are given short-term credit terms (like 'pay within 30 days'). As a result, accounts receivable represents a customer "IOU".

That's why it's important to analyze accounts receivable in detail.

**Accounts receivable turnover** is calculated as revenue divided by the average accounts receivable balance <u>This metric calculates how often the average receivable balance at the Company is collected throughout the year.</u>

$$\text{Receivables Turnover:} \frac{\text{Revenue}}{\text{Average Receivables}}$$

A receivable turnover ratio of 10, means the average receivable balance is collected 10 times throughout the period.

<u>A higher receivable turnover ratio is more desirable</u> because it means the business converts receivables (IOUs from

customers) to cash faster.

Say we wanted to figure out how long it took the company to collect on its receivables due from customers. This brings us to the calculation of "days sales outstanding" or DSO.

**DSO is calculated as the number of days in the period divided by the accounts receivable turnover ratio.**

$$\text{Days Sales Outstanding (DSO): } \frac{\text{\# of days in period}}{\text{Receivables Turnover}}$$

If we were comparing annual figures, the days in the period would be 365. Similarly, if we were comparing quarterly figures, the days in the period would be 90 days.

A DSO of 30 days means that the average accounts receivable balance is collected in 30 days.

This is an important figure to analyze because it shows how fast a business is able to convert receivables to cash. The faster the collection period, the better.

Typically, analysts compare accounts receivable turnover and DSO relative to prior year results. If DSO increased, we would want to figure out why.

For instance, did the Company extend payment terms to customers? Did they have trouble collecting from financially troubled customers?

Conversely, if DSO declined, we would want to figure out why. Did the company incentivize customers to pay early? Did the company do a better job of identifying troublesome customers?

**Inventory Turnover**

Inventory turnover is a similar metric to receivable turnover.

**Inventory turnover** is calculated as cost of goods sold divided by average inventory. It calculates how often the average inventory balance is sold during the period.

$$\text{Inventory Turnover:} \frac{\text{Cost of Goods Sold}}{\text{Average Inventory}}$$

An inventory turnover ratio of 15 means the average inventory balance is sold 15 times during the period.

A higher inventory turnover is more desirable because it means the business is able to convert merchandise inventory into sales (and thus cash) faster.

Another important metric to consider is determining how long it takes the company to sell its average inventory balance. This is referred to as 'days sales of inventory' or DSI.

DSI is calculated as the number of days in the period divided by inventory turnover.

$$\text{Days Sales of Inventory (DSI):} \frac{\text{\# of days in period}}{\text{Inventory Turnover}}$$

A DSI of 60 days means it takes the company 60 days on average to sell its inventory.

DSI is a closely followed metric because if a business has too much inventory, it may have mis-forecasted demand. As a result, a multi-period increase in DSI should be closely followed with additional research.

## Accounts Payable Turnover

The final turnover metric we'll look at is accounts payable turnover. Accounts payable represents obligations to pay vendors for purchases on credit.

**Accounts payable turnover** is calculated as cost of goods sold divided by average accounts payable.

Accounts payable turnover shows how many times the average vendor payable balance is paid during the period. A ratio of 10 means the average accounts payable balance is paid 10 times throughout the period.

Similar to the other turnover metrics, it is often a good idea to calculate how long it takes a business to pay its average payables balance. This is referred to as 'days payable outstanding' or DPO.

DPO is calculated as the number of days in the period divided by payable turnover.

**DPO effectively shows how long it takes a business to pay its suppliers/vendors.** For instance, a DPO of 30 means that the business pays its suppliers within 30 days on average.

Once DSO, DSI, and DPO have been calculated, we have a much better understanding of how fast the company generates cash. We can take these metrics one step further by calculating the cash conversion cycle.

The cash conversion cycle is calculated as DSI plus DSO less DPO.

**The cash conversion cycle tells investors how many days it takes the company to purchase inventory, repay vendors, and collect receivables from sales to customers.**

<u>Obviously, a lower cash conversion cycle is desired because it means the business will be able to convert its assets to cash faster.</u>

**Return On Assets**

In business, we often want to get a certain return on our investments. This is why return analysis is a crucial part of financial statement analysis. <u>Return analysis just refers to the percentage return we get back for every dollar of investment.</u>

Let's consider return on assets first.

**Return on assets (ROA)** is calculated as net income divided by average assets. By average assets, I mean the average balance over past two periods.

$$\text{Return On Assets:} \frac{\text{Net Income}}{\text{Average Assets}}$$

<u>Return on assets measures the return the company generates (i.e. profit) for every dollar invested in assets.</u>

A return on assets of 20% means the business generates 20 cents of profit for every dollar invested in its assets.

Return on assets can actually be broken down even further through simple math. Return on assets can also be calculated as profit margin multiplied against asset turnover.

$$\text{Return On Assets:} \frac{\text{Net Income}}{\text{Revenue}} \times \frac{\text{Revenue}}{\text{Average Assets}}$$

Remember, profit margin (also known as net margin) represents net income over sales. Profit margin tells investors how much the company brings home in profit for every dollar of sales generated.

Meanwhile, asset turnover measures how efficiently the Company uses its assets to generate sales.

The main reason to look at the break down of the ROA formula is to better understand how the company uses its assets to generate profit.

Some companies have very low asset turnover ratios, but make up for it with higher margins. An example of would be a jewelry store. Jewelry stores turnover (sell) inventory very slowly, but each sale has a very high margin.

Other companies might have high asset turnovers and low profit margins. An example of this would be grocery stores. Grocery stores don't make too much profit per item sold, however, they make up for it with a ton of volume.

**Return On Equity**

As analysts we want to know the amount of profit the company generates from the capital investors have invested into the business. In other words, we want to know the return on equity.

**Return on equity (ROE)** is calculated as net income divided by average equity.

$$\text{Return On Equity:} \frac{\text{Net Income}}{\text{Average Equity}}$$

Remember equity represents (1) the amount of cash investors have invested into the company and (2) any profits that have been reinvested in the business.

ROE measures how much profit the business generates for every dollar investors have invested and/or reinvested in the business.

For instance, a return of equity of 20% means the business generates 20 cents of profit for every dollar investors have invested/re-invested into the company.

Obviously, a higher ROE is more desirable.

ROE is a very famous metric because it can be broken down into smaller components. This is referred as the **DuPont framework or DuPont analysis.**

This method to measure profitability was pioneered by the DuPont Corporation in the 1920s. And it is still used in corporate finance today.

The DuPont formula breaks down the return on equity formula into return on assets and an equity multiplier. As we discussed previously, return on assets can be broken down into profit margin multiplied against asset turnover.

$$\textbf{Return On Equity: } \frac{\text{Net Income}}{\text{Revenue}} \text{ X } \frac{\text{Revenue}}{\text{Average Assets}} \text{ X } \frac{\text{Average Assets}}{\text{Average Equity}}$$

**As a result, the three components of the DuPont formula are**

**(1) profitability, (2) asset activity, and (3) financial leverage.**

Financial leverage just refers to the amount of debt on the company's balance sheet. **Financial leverage** in this case is calculated as total assets divided by total equity.

Through the DuPont formula, we can see how a company is able to generate higher ROE through:

*higher margin per dollar of sales

*faster turnover of assets

*and/or higher financial leverage.

**Keep in mind that there are trade-offs with all three components.** Increasing leverage can increase profits. However, too much debt can put the Company at risk of bankruptcy.

## Liquidity Ratios

Liquidity refers to how easy it is to convert assets to cash. Assets such as accounts receivable are typically much easier to convert to cash than long-term assets such as office buildings.

The purpose of liquidity analysis is to determine if the company can meet its short-term obligations. The most common method to evaluate short-term liquidity is through the current ratio.

**The current ratio is calculated as current assets over current liabilities.**

$$\text{Current Ratio:} \frac{\text{Current Assets}}{\text{Current Liabilities}}$$

Remember, current assets are assets that will be utilized within one year and current liabilities are liabilities that will be paid (or settled) within one year.

If the current ratio is greater than 1, it typically signals a healthy ability to meet short-term obligations. The higher the current ratio, the more capable the Company is of paying its short-term obligations.

If the current ratio is less than one, it may signal that the company may need to rely on long-term credit financing or issuing equity to fund cash shortfalls...or in the worst case, run into a liquidity crunch (i.e. bankruptcy).

Some analysts like to modify the current ratio to only consider current assets that are readily available to convert to cash. The modified ratio is known as the **acid test ratio or the quick ratio.**

The ratio excludes inventories and prepaid items from current assets. This is because these items are typically harder to convert to cash.

As a result, the numerator only consists of 'quick assets', which includes cash, short-term investments, and accounts receivable. The denominator is still the same, which is current liabilities.

Hence, the quick ratio is a more conservative calculation of a company's ability to meet short-term obligations.

**Leverage Analysis**

Aside from the ability to meet short-term obligations, shareholders should also be concerned about a company's long-term solvency. Leverage ratios are used to determine a company's ability to repay its long-term debt.

One commonly used metric to assess leverage is called the **interest coverage ratio.**

It is calculated as Net income before interest expense and income taxes divided by interest expense.

$$\text{Interest Coverage Ratio:} \frac{\text{Net Income} + \text{Interest Expense} + \text{Taxes}}{\text{Interest Expense}}$$

The metric measures how easily a business can pay periodic interest expense on outstanding debt with available earnings.

A higher interest coverage ratio means the company has a higher ability to pay interest on its debts.

Generally speaking, an interest coverage ratio of less than

one is very concerning because it means the Company is unable to cover basic interest expense (let alone principal repayment). In such a scenario, bankruptcy is a very likely scenario.

Another commonly used metric is debt-to-equity.

**Debt-to-equity** is calculated as total liabilities divided by total shareholder's equity.

$$\text{Debt-to-Equity Ratio:} \frac{\text{Debt}}{\text{Equity}}$$

This measures how much debt is used to finance assets relative to the amount shareholders have invested in the business.

All else equal, the higher the debt-to-equity ratio, the higher the risk of insolvency. Conversely, a lower debt-to-equity ratio implies a more financially stable business.

The other popular leverage ratio used by investors is debt-to-EBITDA. In fact, this is a commonly used metric by banks and credit agencies to assess a company's likelihood of defaulting on debt.

It is calculated as debt divided by EBITDA. EBITDA simply represents net income before interest, taxes, depreciation expense, and amortization expense.

Analysts use debt-to-EBITDA to measure how well a company can cover its debts based on earnings. A higher ratio means the company has more debt per dollar of earnings. A lower ratio generally suggests a more financially stable business.

**Keep in mind that different industries have different benchmarks for leverage.** Some industries like retail stores hardly use any debt, while it may be very common for companies in the casino industry to use a ton of leverage.

## Valuation Ratios

Valuation ratios are metrics analysts use to assess how expensive or cheap a business is.

The first valuation metric we'll look at is price-to-earnings ratio also known as the PE ratio. **The PE ratio is calculated as the stock price divided by earnings per share (on a diluted basis).** Remember, earnings per share simply represents net income divided by shares outstanding.

$$\text{Price-To-Earnings (P/E) Ratio:} \frac{\text{Stock Price}}{\text{EPS}}$$

PE measures how much investors are paying for a business relative to its profits. For instance, a PE ratio of 15 means that investors are willing to pay $15 to purchase the company's stock for every dollar of profit it generates.

Higher quality companies typically trade for higher PE multiples and lower quality companies trade at lower multiples.

Sometimes analysts like to use a forward P/E ratio. This differs from the normal P/E ratio because the earnings are based on forecasted earnings instead of past historical earnings. **The forward P/E measures how expensive or cheap a stock is relative to future earnings forecast expectations.**

Sometimes investors like to measure valuation based on cash flow instead of net income. This is because net income is an accounting output that may include non-cash expenses such as depreciation expense. Hence, some believe cash flow is a more appropriate measure to value a business.

**Price-to-Cash Flow (P/CF)**

**Price-to-cash flow is calculated as the company's market capitalization divided by cash from operating activities.**

$$\text{Price-To-Cash Flow (P/CF) Ratio:} \frac{\text{Market Capitalization}}{\text{Cash from Operations}}$$

Market capitalization just refers to dollar market value of a company's shares (i.e. share count x share price).

<u>Price to cash flow measures how much investors are willing to pay for a business relative to the cash flow it generates.</u>

A price-to-cash flow ratio of 20 means investors are willing to pay $20 per dollar of cash flow the business generates.

**Price-to-Sales (P/S)**

Sometimes a business is not generating positive net income or cash flow because it's a start up or because it is investing heavily to drive sales growth.

As a result, PE and price-to-cash flow are not good metrics to evaluate these kinds of businesses. This is particularly common in high growth technology companies.

Instead, we evaluate how expensive or cheap these companies are based on sales. **Price-to-sales (aka P/S) is calculated as the market capitalization of the business divided by sales over the past twelve months.**

$$\text{Price-To-Sales (P/S) Ratio: } \frac{\text{Market Capitalization}}{\text{Sales}}$$

<u>Price-to-sales measures how much investors are willing to pay for the business for every dollar of sales generated.</u>

A price to sales ratio of 2x means that investors are willing to pay $2 for every dollar of sales the business generates.

**Price-to-Book (P/B)**

Before we move onto the next valuation metric, let's first define a few terms. Book value is a very important tool in financial analysis. It represents the net assets of a business (i.e. total assets less total liabilities). It is the theoretical value of a business if it were liquidated.

Book value per share represents the book value of the company divided by the diluted share count.

One metric analysts utilize in certain industries is **price-**

**to-book (P/B) ratio**. This is calculated as the company's share price divided by book value per share.

P/B measures how much investors are paying for the net assets of a business. It also provides a sense of how much protection investors have if the business went bankrupt.

<u>Price-to-book is a useful metric for businesses with primarily tangible assets such as a manufacturing business or a bank or even an insurance company.</u>

It is less useful to evaluate companies that rely heavily on intangible assets such as technology companies or pharmaceuticals.

**Enterprise Value**

The final valuation metric we'll look at is enterprise value (EV).

Recall that the market capitalization is the dollar market value of a company's outstanding shares. Some analysts like to use enterprise value instead because it takes into account the level of debt the business has.

Enterprise value is calculated as market capitalization plus preferred shares plus debt plus minority interests less cash.

A commonly used valuation multiple is Enterprise value-to-EBITDA (EV/EBITDA). EV/EBITDA measures the multiple a potential acquirer might pay for a business.

In the event of a buyout, the acquirer would generally (1) pay for the fair value of the Company, (2) take on the company's debt, and (3) receive any cash on the acquiree's balance sheet.

An EV/EBITDA multiple of 7 means that a potential acquirer would be essentially paying $7 for every dollar of profit the business generates.

A higher EV/EBITDA ratio means that a potential acquirer would have to pay more to acquire the business for every dollar of profit earned.

# How To Read Financial Statements

A lot of people think financial statement analysis is all about calculating financial ratios and other metrics. However, it requires much more than crunching a few numbers.

**To be a great analyst, you need to be able to read SEC filings and financial statements like the back of your hand.**

I'm going to teach how to read the most popular financial filings and what information to look for so you don't miss anything important.

All public companies in the U.S. are required to file documents with the Securities and Exchange Commission also known as the SEC.  These filings are made available to the public for free.

You can access these filings on the SEC's website (https://www.sec.gov/edgar/searchedgar/companysearch.html).

First, let's go through a quick overview of the key SEC filings you need to be able to read.

*The first is the 10-K. This is a company's annual report filed with the SEC detailing its financial performance over the past year.

*A 10-Q is similar to the 10-K, but it only reports a company's financial performance over a quarter.

*An 8-K is a broad form used to inform shareholders of key events impacting the Company.

*A DEF-14A is a company's annual proxy statement where important information about insiders is disclosed.

*Finally, we'll also take a look at Form 4's, which detail the share holdings of the company's important insiders.

**Reading the 10-K**

Let's start our analysis with the 10-K. Large companies in the U.S. (which means those with a market capitalization of over $700 million) must file their 10-K with the SEC 60 days after the fiscal year.

**The 10-K is required reading material for any serious investor.**

To get an idea of how important the 10-K is, Warren Buffett, the greatest investor of all time, reportedly reads 500 pages of filings every single day!

A 10-K is a public company's annual report with the SEC detailing its business performance over the past year. A 10-K is not the same thing as the annual report to shareholders.

The annual report to shareholders is usually a professionally designed document delivered to investors. It typically includes a letter from the CEO or Chairman. The annual report will almost always include more graphs, color, and charts than the 10-K.

Many companies just put a CEO letter in front of the 10-K and include a few charts and photos for their annual report.

**The number one reason why you should read the 10-K is that the annual report is usually much more biased than the 10-K.** The annual report is more often than not a marketing tool to retain shareholders or attract new ones.

Peter Lynch, one of the greatest investors, once said:

*"All else being equal, invest in the company with the fewest color photographs in the annual report."*

Reading your first 10-K can be a daunting task, so I'm going to give you a few tips.

The first thing to be aware of is that the reading material is extremely dry. This is not like reading a Stephen King suspense novel.

**For beginners I do not recommend reading a 10-K all in one sitting.** These documents can easily be over 200 pages. Take lots of breaks to remain fresh. The last thing you want to do is skip over an important section, misread something, or misinterpret something.

**For certain sections of the 10-K, I find it best to read the current year 10-K with the prior year 10-K side-by-side.** This way you can better identify if there are any important changes in disclosures or policy. I'll let you know which sections you want to do this as we dissect the components of the 10-K.

☐

**Business Section**

The first part of the 10-K is the business section. **This section briefly describes what the company does.** It may include a description of the products and services, operating segments, competitors, employees, or even discusses the market(s) the company competes in.

The business section may even include a discussion of recent events or regulations impacting the business, labor issues, or potential lawsuits.

As an example, here is part of the business section of Costco's latest 10-K:

**Item 1—Business**

Costco Wholesale Corporation and its subsidiaries (Costco or the Company) began operations in 1983 in Seattle, Washington. We are principally engaged in the operation of membership warehouses in the United States (U.S.) and Puerto Rico, Canada, United Kingdom (U.K.), Mexico, Japan, Australia, Spain, and through majority-owned subsidiaries in Taiwan and Korea. Costco operated 715, 686, and 663 warehouses worldwide at August 28, 2016, August 30, 2015, and August 31, 2014, respectively. Our common stock trades on the NASDAQ Global Select Market, under the symbol "COST."

We report on a 52/53-week fiscal year, consisting of thirteen, four-week periods and ending on the Sunday nearest the end of August. The first three quarters consist of three periods each, and the fourth quarter consists of four periods (five weeks in the thirteenth period in a 53-week year). The material seasonal impact in our operations is an increased level of net sales and earnings during the winter holiday season. References to 2016, 2015, and 2014 relate to the 52-week fiscal years ended August 28, 2016, August 30, 2015, and August 31, 2014, respectively.

## Risk Factors

The risk factors section of the 10-K describes key risks the company faces. These may include factors such as employee strikes, competition, or dependence on a large customer.

**This section tells investors what could go wrong with the company**--so it is very important to read every sentence. <u>I would highly recommend reading the current year 10-K with the prior year 10-K, so you can see if there are any new risk factors.</u>

Keep in mind that the risk factors are often drafted up by lawyers, so the language can be very boilerplate (meaning it may contain very standard language).

It is very common place to see things like: *"if the economy weakens, demand for our products may also be weak."*

Even though the language may be boilerplate, you should

still read through it all because you never know what information you'll come across.

Having read hundreds and thousands of 10-Ks over the years, I have compiled a list of key factors you should watch out for:

**\*Changes in competition**: Companies sometimes list competitors in the risk factors section. It is a good idea to see if any new names pop up. This may signal increased competition in the industry.

**\*Customer concentration**: Any customer that accounts for a significant percentage of sales could be a big risk. I use 10%+ as a threshold.

**\*New/pending regulation**: Any disclosures on new regulations that may impact the business should be read closely.

**\*Any important lawsuits**: If the company is involved in a high-profile lawsuit, the risk factors section should be read to assess the potential risk.

**\*Commentary about debt levels**: If the company is highly levered, anything discussing debt levels in the risk factors should be read.

**\*Dependence on certain products**: Some companies generate a substantial portion of sales from one product (like Apple's iPhone). Any disclosures regarding dependence on a few key products should be closely read.

**\*Dependence on certain suppliers or manufacturers**: Some companies rely on a few suppliers. This can be a big risk if the suppliers want to raise prices or if they go out of business.

This is by no means a comprehensive list, but it's a great checklist to keep in mind when you're reading through the risk factors.

**Unresolved Staff Comments**

The unresolved staff comments section of the 10-K requires companies to explain comments it received from the SEC on previously filed reports that have not been resolved.

**If you see any comments in this section, it should be taken as a red flag and investigated further**. Most companies leave this part blank because there are no unresolved staff comments--

it is a very rare occurrence.

## Properties

The properties section of the 10-K details information about the company's significant properties. This may include its store locations, headquarters, manufacturing plants, and/or sales office locations. <u>This can be useful in analysis if you're trying to see what geographic locations the company is expanding in.</u>

As an example, this is a portion of Costco's properties disclosure from its latest 10-K:

**Warehouse Properties**

At August 28, 2016 we operated 715 membership warehouses:

### NUMBER OF WAREHOUSES

| | Own Land and Building | Lease Land and/or Building(1) | Total |
|---|---|---|---|
| United States and Puerto Rico | 407 | 94 | 501 |
| Canada | 80 | 11 | 91 |
| Mexico | 36 | — | 36 |
| United Kingdom | 22 | 6 | 28 |
| Japan | 11 | 14 | 25 |
| Korea | 5 | 7 | 12 |
| Taiwan | — | 12 | 12 |
| Australia | 5 | 3 | 8 |
| Spain | 2 | — | 2 |
| Total | 568 | 147 | 715 |

## Legal Proceedings

The legal proceedings section of the 10-K describes all of its important legal issues. The language may be boilerplate, but it can help identify key risks to watch out for! The disclosure will differ across companies, but most will give you a detailed timeline of the legal matter, including any settlement determinations.

If you know the company is involved in a high-profile legal matter, this would be the place to dig up some additional information.

**Item 5**

Item 5 of the 10-K is a short section summarizing information about the company's shares. This typically includes a very brief table about the share price, dividends, or share repurchases.

It is a great section to go through if you want quick information about the shares, especially to see if the share count has increased.

Here is part of Costco's Item 5 disclosure from the latest 10-K:

| | Price Range | | Cash Dividends Declared |
|---|---|---|---|
| | High | Low | |
| **2016:** | | | |
| Fourth Quarter | $  169.04 | $  141.29 | $  0.450 |
| Third Quarter | 158.25 | 146.44 | 0.450 |
| Second Quarter | 168.87 | 143.28 | 0.400 |
| First Quarter | 163.10 | 138.30 | 0.400 |
| **2015:** | | | |
| Fourth Quarter | 146.89 | 132.71 | 0.400 |
| Third Quarter | 153.14 | 143.05 | 0.400 |
| Second Quarter | 155.92 | 137.31 | 5.355 |
| First Quarter | 140.01 | 121.35 | 0.355 |

## Selected Financial Data

All large companies are required to disclose "selected financial data" in the 10-K over the past five years. Companies typically disclose important income statement figures and balance sheet accounts, along with other key performance metrics.

This section is a great way to get a quick look and see how the company performed over the past few years.

Here is part of Costco's selected financial data table from the latest 10-K:

| SELECTED FINANCIAL DATA (dollars in millions, except per share data) | | | | | |
|---|---|---|---|---|---|
| As of and for the year ended | Aug. 28, 2016 (52 weeks) | Aug. 30, 2015 (52 weeks) | Aug. 31, 2014 (52 weeks) | Sept. 1, 2013 (52 weeks) | Sept. 2, 2012 (53 weeks) |
| **RESULTS OF OPERATIONS** | | | | | |
| Net sales | $ 116,073 | $ 113,666 | $ 110,212 | $ 102,870 | $ 97,062 |
| Membership fees | 2,646 | 2,533 | 2,428 | 2,286 | 2,075 |
| Gross margin[1] as a percentage of net sales | 11.35 % | 11.09 % | 10.66% | 10.62% | 10.55% |
| Selling, general and administrative expenses as a percentage of net sales | 10.40 % | 10.07 % | 9.89% | 9.82% | 9.81% |
| Operating income | $ 3,672 | $ 3,624 | $ 3,220 | $ 3,053 | $ 2,759 |
| Net income attributable to Costco[2] | 2,350 | 2,377 | 2,058 | 2,039 | 1,709 |
| Net income per diluted common share attributable to Costco | 5.33 | 5.37 | 4.65 | 4.63 | 3.89 |
| Cash dividends declared per common share | 1.70 | 6.51 | 1.33 | 8.17 | 1.03 |
| Changes in comparable sales[3] | | | | | |
| United States | 1 % | 3 % | 5% | 6% | 7% |
| Canada | (3)% | (5)% | 2% | 9% | 8% |
| Other International | (3)% | (3)% | 3% | 1% | 3% |
| Total Company | 0 % | 1 % | 4% | 6% | 7% |

## Management's Discussion and Analysis

The management's discussion and analysis (MD&A) section of the 10-K is important reading material for all investors. The section typically begins with a discussion of the year's financial highlights and commentary about the ongoing strategy.

If you're just researching the company for the first time, this is a great section to read to get the basic highlights over the past year.

The MD&A will also discuss certain financial metrics (including the results of its income statement over the past three years) on a line-by-line basis.

The MD&A commentary differs between companies, but it

typically includes a discussion of why revenue increased or decreased, why profit increased or decreased, certain one-time expenses incurred, and about taxes.

**It is important to read the MD&A to get more detail about results that may not be apparent from just looking at the numbers.**

The next section of the MD&A focuses on liquidity and capital resources.

Here, the company discusses significant inflows and outflows of cash. In other words it will include a discussion about each section of the statement of cash flows.

<u>This is important to read in order to get a better understanding of how the company is generating cash, what it is investing in, and how it is financing the business.</u>

In this section of the MD&A, the company may also elect to discuss available credit resources. This includes a discussion of who the Company's bank is, what the borrowing limit is, interest rates, and any financial covenants.

Companies are also required to include a table on contractual obligations. This represents any future large outflows of cash it has already committed to.  These obligations may include debt, purchase obligations, and lease/rent obligations, or inventory purchase commitments.

This is the contractual obligations table from Costco's latest 10-K:

**Contractual Obligations**

As of August 28, 2016, our commitments to make future payments under contractual obligations were as follows:

| | Payments Due by Fiscal Year | | | | |
|---|---|---|---|---|---|
| Contractual obligations | 2017 | 2018 to 2019 | 2020 to 2021 | 2022 and thereafter | Total |
| Purchase obligations (merchandise)[1] | $ 5,833 | $ 3 | $ — | $ — | $ 5,836 |
| Long-term debt[2] | 1,221 | 1,392 | 1,845 | 998 | 5,456 |
| Operating leases [3] | 200 | 379 | 337 | 2,204 | 3,120 |
| Construction and land obligations | 700 | 57 | — | — | 757 |
| Capital lease obligations[4] | 31 | 61 | 63 | 593 | 748 |
| Purchase obligations (equipment, services and other)[5] | 458 | 98 | 61 | 1 | 618 |
| Other[6] | 18 | 26 | 11 | 71 | 126 |
| Total | $ 8,461 | $ 2,016 | $ 2,317 | $ 3,867 | $ 16,661 |

Finally, at the end of the MD&A, the company is required to discuss its critical accounting policies. These are policies that can significantly influence its financial results and/or financial position.

These policies typically include discussion of revenue recognition, inventory valuation, impairment analysis, and income taxes.

The disclosures here are very similar to disclosures we will encounter in the financial statement footnotes.

**Item 7A**

Item 7A of the 10-K discusses various market risks the company faces. Market risks refers to risks the company is not entirely in control of.

**This includes interest rates, foreign currency, and commodity prices.** The company is required to discuss how these risks impact the business and how it mitigates them.

If you're researching a company that generates substantial revenue in a foreign country, or is highly levered with debt, or depends on a single commodity, this would be a very important section to read.

**Item 8**

Item 8 of the 10-K discloses the actual financial statements and certain other supplementary data. It will also include the audit opinion, which is very important!

All public companies are required to have an independent auditor. This is to ensure the financials are accurately stated so users can make informed decisions. Having an auditor doesn't eliminate the risk of fraud, but it reduces it significantly.

Most large companies select one of the big 4 auditors:

*Ernst and Young also known as EY,

*PricewaterhouseCoopers also known as PwC,

*Deloitte, and

*KPMG.

**The 10-K must disclose the independent auditor's audit opinion regarding (1) the fairness of the financials presented and (2) the effectiveness of the company's internal controls.**

Fairness of the financials presented refers to whether or not they are presented without any significant mistakes and errors and in accordance with U.S. Generally Accepted Accounting Principles (GAAP).

The opinion over internal controls refers to the company's processes to ensure operational effectiveness and efficiency, reliable financial reporting, and compliance with internal and external laws, regulations, and policies.

In other words, internal controls refers to the processes put in place to ensure the integrity of accounting and financial information presented and the application of various rules and regulation.

Most companies will receive an "unqualified opinion" on the audit, which is also known as a 'clean opinion'. This means the auditor believes the (1) financial statements are free of material misstatements and (2) that the internal controls are effective.

**If an opinion other than an unqualified opinion is given, it would be taken as a red flag.** Sometimes it is because the company has poor controls over its accounting and finance processes. This may result in improperly reported numbers or in the worst case financial fraud.

In general it is best to avoid investing in companies that do not have clean audits.

After the audit opinion has been disclosed, the financial

statements follow. The 10-K will disclose (1) a balance sheet for the last two years and (2) the income statement, the statement of stockholder's equity, and statement of cash flows for the past 3 years.

After the financial statements have been presented, the footnotes follow. **The footnotes are often the most important section of the 10-K to read.** <u>They include a variety of details about the company's account balances and accounting policies.</u>

I highly recommend reading the footnotes section from the latest 10-K side-by-side with the prior year 10-K. This way you can see if there are any changes in disclosure that are important.

**The 10-K Footnotes**

There are a few footnote sections that are more important than others. We'll discuss the most important ones.

The first section to read is revenue recognition. **This details how the company recognizes sales/revenue.**

Sales can be recognized under a variety of scenarios

including:

*When the product is delivered to the customer

*Based on some kind of estimate of hours worked on a service project

*Or it can even be recognized over a subscription service period.

You definitely want to know how a company recognizes its sales! It is best to compare the current year's revenue recognition disclosure with the prior year to see if any policies changed.

Another important footnote disclosure to read is the one about accounts receivable. Remember, these are IOUs from customers.

The level of accounts receivable disclosure will vary by company. Some companies actually provide investors with an aging schedule for the receivables.

**An aging schedule is a table that details how long receivables have been outstanding from customers and if any are past due (i.e. late).**

Obviously, if there is a big increase in past due receivables, that might warrant a bit more research.

Check out Cisco's aging schedule disclosure from its latest 10-K:

| July 30, 2016 | | DAYS PAST DUE (INCLUDES BILLED AND UNBILLED) | | | | | | | | Current |
|---|---|---|---|---|---|---|---|---|---|---|
| | | 31 - 60 | | 61 - 90 | | 91+ | | Total Past Due | | |
| Lease receivables | $ | 111 | $ | 25 | $ | 251 | $ | 387 | $ | 2,711 |
| Loan receivables | | 30 | | 9 | | 37 | | 76 | | 2,059 |
| Financed service contracts and other | | 213 | | 152 | | 565 | | 930 | | 2,440 |
| Total | $ | 354 | $ | 186 | $ | 853 | $ | 1,393 | $ | 7,210 |

Inventory disclosures are also important to read up on, specifically regarding inventory valuation policies.

The important thing to read about is whether the company wrote off any obsolete inventory. In many cases, companies write off inventory because they have too much and will never be able to sell through it all.

Also, keep an eye out for a large inventory build. If demand has been robust, it is unlikely inventory would pile up.

The property, plant, and equipment (PP&E) section is also important to review. Companies will typically provide a breakdown of PP&E under various categories such as buildings, machinery, furniture and fixtures, computer hardware, and others.

Check out Cisco's disclosure of its PP&E in its latest 10-K:

| Property and equipment, net: | | | | |
|---|---|---|---|---|
| Gross property and equipment: | | | | |
| Land, buildings, and building and leasehold improvements | $ | 4,778 | $ | 4,495 |
| Computer equipment and related software | | 1,288 | | 1,310 |
| Production, engineering, and other equipment | | 5,658 | | 5,753 |
| Operating lease assets | | 296 | | 372 |
| Furniture and fixtures | | 543 | | 497 |
| Total gross property and equipment | | 12,563 | | 12,427 |
| Less: accumulated depreciation and amortization | | (9,057) | | (9,095) |
| Total | $ | 3,506 | $ | 3,332 |

Many will disclose the useful life of its PP&E. This represents the period of time over which the company will recognize the expense for the cost of equipment (also known as depreciation expense).

It would be a good idea to check if the useful life ranges have changed. Remember, if the useful life increased, that means the company is recognizing less expense every year (i.e. a potential benefit).

If the company has a high level of debt, it would smart to read through the footnotes on debt.

Companies will disclose a wealth of information on their debt including the amount outstanding, interest rates, debt maturity, financial covenants, and other pertinent information. These are very important disclosures to evaluate the health of the business.

Check out Costco's useful footnote detailing all of its debt from the latest 10-K:

| | 2016 | | 2015 | |
|---|---|---|---|---|
| | Carrying Value | Fair Value | Carrying Value | Fair Value |
| 0.65% Senior Notes due December 2015 | $ 0 | $ 0 | $ 1,200 | $ 1,201 |
| 5.5% Senior Notes due March 2017 | 1,100 | 1,129 | 1,099 | 1,171 |
| 1.125% Senior Notes due December 2017 | 1,099 | 1,103 | 1,098 | 1,097 |
| 1.7% Senior Notes due December 2019 | 1,196 | 1,219 | 1,195 | 1,186 |
| 1.75% Senior Notes due February 2020 | 498 | 508 | 497 | 494 |
| 2.25% Senior Notes due February 2022 | 497 | 512 | 496 | 484 |
| Other long-term debt | 771 | 803 | 550 | 555 |
| Total long-term debt | 5,161 | 5,274 | 6,135 | 6,188 |
| Less current portion | 1,100 | 1,130 | 1,283 | 1,284 |
| Long-term debt, excluding current portion | $ 4,061 | $ 4,144 | $ 4,852 | $ 4,904 |

Acquisition footnotes are important to review. The level of disclosure varies, but it may briefly discuss why they made an acquisition and the strategy for that business going forward.

Other pertinent information such as the purchase price should be disclosed. Some companies will even provide the amount of revenue and profit contribution from acquired businesses.

This is critical if you want to calculate an organic growth figure (we'll discuss this later).

Finally, the last section you would want to review in the footnotes on taxes. Obviously, taxes are very complex and I am by no means an expert.

However, the tax footnote disclosure is still worth reading. For instance, you may want to know how much net operating loss carryforwards a company has to offset future profits...or maybe you want to know what the company's uncertain tax position is with the IRS.

Further, most companies will disclose how its effective tax rate is different than the statutory tax rate (which is 35% in the U.S.). This may be important to read if the company has an unusually low (or high) tax rate.

Costco provides a similar disclosure in its latest 10-K:

The reconciliation between the statutory tax rate and the effective rate for 2016, 2015, and 2014 is as follows:

|  | 2016 | | 2015 | |
|---|---|---|---|---|
| Federal taxes at statutory rate | $ 1,267 | 35.0 % | $ 1,262 | 35.0 % |
| State taxes, net | 91 | 2.5 | 85 | 2.3 |
| Foreign taxes, net | (21) | (0.6) | (125) | (3.5) |
| Employee stock ownership plan (ESOP) | (17) | (0.5) | (66) | (1.8) |
| Other | (77) | (2.1) | 39 | 1.2 |
| Total | $ 1,243 | 34.3 % | $ 1,195 | 33.2 % |

## Other Key Footnote Disclosures

Some other key footnote disclosures to read are located near the end of the 10-K. The first is segment reporting. Segments are the smaller business units of the company that the management team uses to evaluate performance. Segments are often split by major product lines, product groups, or even by geography.

The segment reporting disclosure typically displays segment revenue and various profit. This may be helpful especially if the Company has businesses in multiple industries.

Check out Costco's segment disclosure from the latest 10-K:

| | United States Operations | Canadian Operations | Other International Operations | Total |
|---|---|---|---|---|
| **2016** | | | | |
| Total revenue | $ 86,579 | $ 17,028 | $ 15,112 | $ 118,719 |
| Operating income | 2,326 | 778 | 568 | 3,672 |
| Depreciation and amortization | 946 | 109 | 200 | 1,255 |
| Additions to property and equipment | 1,823 | 299 | 527 | 2,649 |
| Net property and equipment | 11,745 | 1,628 | 3,670 | 17,043 |
| Total assets | 22,511 | 3,480 | 7,172 | 33,163 |

Companies are also required to disclose geographic information to the SEC. Near the end of the 10-K, companies will have a few tables disclosing revenue and assets by geography. This is helpful to understand what geographic regions are important.

Reading the footnotes of the 10-K is very important for serious investors. The footnotes can certainly be dry reading material.

As a result, I highly recommend taking multiple breaks so your mind stays fresh and you don't miss any important disclosures.

**Reading the 10-Q (Quarterly Report)**

Public companies in the U.S. are required to file periodic reports with the SEC. We've already covered the most important one, the 10-K.

In the U.S. companies are required to file quarterly reports with the SEC. These are referred to as the 10-Q.

A 10-Q must be filed with the SEC 40 days after the end of the quarter. **The 10-Q is a much shorter filing than the 10-K and it details financial results and certain disclosures about the quarter.**

The financial statements are the first things disclosed in the 10-Q and include:

*The balance sheet as of the latest quarter and the most recent fiscal year end.

*The income statement for both (1) the current quarter/prior year and (2) on a year-to-date basis.

*The year-to-date statement of cash flows for the current

year and prior year.

After the financials have been presented, the 10-Q footnotes follow. The footnotes in the 10-Q are often abbreviated and have less disclosure than the 10-K.

Some footnotes may only be presented on an annual basis in the 10-K and not disclosed on a quarterly basis in the 10-Q. Nevertheless, it is still important to read through all of the footnotes in the 10-Q.

After the footnotes, the 10-Q also contains a management's discussion and analysis or MD&A section. This is the same disclosure from the 10-K.

Remember, the MD&A disclosures will discuss recent results and provide some commentary about business performance. **It is important to read the MD&A to get a better understanding of the financial performance that may not be evident from just looking at the numbers.**

# Reading the 8-K

An 8-K also known as the "current report" is filed with the SEC to announce major events shareholders should know about.

An 8-K can virtually be filed about anything including the following items:

*Acquisitions: If the company acquired another business, an 8-K should be filed detailing the terms of the transaction such as purchase price, expected contribution (i.e. revenue/profit) to results, and when the acquisition is expected to close.

*Business divestitures: If the company sold a business, that should be disclosed in an 8-K filings with details regarding the terms of the transaction.

*Quarterly results: Quarterly results are always disclosed in a current report. The report should include company commentary and abbreviated financials.

*Financing: If the company is raising any debt or equity, the terms and pricing of the transaction should be disclosed.

**\*Restructuring plans**: Typically, large restructuring plans are communicated to shareholders. These involve layoffs in order to cut costs. Some companies will even disclose the cost of the restructuring plan and how much money they expect to save.

**\*Change in auditor**: This is a very important event. When it happens, it should be properly communicated with the SEC and investors. The company is also required to disclose if there were any disagreements with the auditor. If there were any disagreements, that should be taken as a red flag.

**\*Executive changes**: Any senior officer changes should be reported in an 8-K. By senior I mean executives in the C-suite such as the chief executive officer, chief financial officer, or the chief operating officer (although sometime changes at the vice president level are also disclosed). The same rule applies if there are any changes to the board of directors.

## Proxy Statement

All public companies are required to file a proxy statement ahead of their annual shareholder's meeting. The proxy statement is also known as form DEF-14A with the SEC.

**The proxy statement discloses pertinent information about the annual meeting, including voting procedure, background about directors and management, and compensation.** This is another key SEC filing to read for all serious investors!

The first section of the proxy is the notice of the annual meeting of shareholders. This details the who, what, where, and when of the meeting.

Check out the notice of the annual meeting from Costco's latest proxy statement:

TO OUR SHAREHOLDERS:

The Annual Meeting of the Shareholders of Costco Wholesale Corporation (the "Company") will be held at the Meydenbauer Center, Center Hall, 11100 N.E. 6th Street, Bellevue, Washington 98004, on Thursday, January 26, 2017, at 4:00 p.m., for the following purposes:

1. To elect the four Class III directors nominated by the Board of Directors to hold office until the 2020 Annual Meeting of Shareholders and until their successors are elected and qualified;

2. To ratify the selection of KPMG LLP ("KPMG") as the Company's independent auditors for fiscal year 2017;

3. To approve, on an advisory basis, the compensation of the Company's executive officers for fiscal year 2016 as disclosed in these materials;

4. To approve, on an advisory basis, the frequency of holding an advisory vote on executive compensation; and

5. To transact such other business as may properly come before the meeting or any adjournments thereof.

The next section is the actual proxy solicitation, which

details what is being voted on at the meeting (including directors standing for election). The proxy will have a background on each of the directors, which includes their business accomplishments.

The Proxy also discuss the role of the various board committees. Companies typically have three board committees: (1) the audit committee, (2) the nominating committee, and (3) the compensation committee.

The audit committee oversees the company's accounting functions to make sure everything is running smoothly. They also engage with the company's independent auditors.

The nominating committee is responsible for selecting potential nominees to become directors. They may also be in charge of corporate governance to make sure proper ethics policies are in place.

Finally, the compensation committee is responsible for awarding compensation to the management team.

**All annual proxy statements contain important information about beneficial ownership**. Beneficial ownership just means how many shares each insider owns.

As shareholders, we want to know if management has skin in the game. The proxy will have a beneficial ownership table disclosing how many shares every single director and management team member owns.

It will also disclose any significant shareholders who own more than 5.0% of the Company.

Take a look at Costco's beneficial ownership disclosure from the latest proxy:

| Name of Beneficial Owner | Shares Beneficially Owned[1] | Percent of Class[2] |
|---|---|---|
| Jeffrey H. Brotman | 463,747[3] | * |
| W. Craig Jelinek | 288,942[4] | * |
| Susan L. Decker | 50,165 | * |
| Daniel J. Evans | 32,604[5] | * |
| Richard A. Galanti | 40,539[6] | * |
| Hamilton E. James | 36,024 | * |
| Richard M. Libenson | 102,044[7] | * |
| John W. Meisenbach | 56,834[8] | * |
| Charles T. Munger | 181,401[9] | * |
| Joseph P. Portera | 26,426[10] | * |
| Jeffrey S. Raikes | 30,054 | * |
| James D. Sinegal | 1,527,207[11] | * |
| John W. Stanton | 17,673[12] | * |
| Mary Agnes (Maggie) Wilderotter | 4,332 | * |
| Dennis R. Zook | 19,694 | * |
| All directors and executive officers as a group (24 persons) | 3,276,400 | * |

Another important thing to consider is how much and how directors and management are compensated. If they were solely paid on sales, a management team may do whatever possible to grow revenue at the expense of profits.

Let's start off with the directors. Directors are typically paid through a combination of an annual cash retainer and equity awards. The proxy will have a table that discloses director compensation.

Here is Costco's disclosure from the latest proxy statement:

The following table summarizes compensation for the non-employee directors of the Company for fiscal 2016.

| Name | Fees Earned or Paid in Cash ($)[1] | Stock Awards ($)[2] | All Other Compensation ($)[3] | Total ($) |
|---|---|---|---|---|
| Susan L. Decker | 42,000 | 332,014 | | 374,014 |
| Daniel J. Evans | 44,000 | 332,014 | | 376,014 |
| Hamilton E. James | 35,000 | 332,014 | | 367,014 |
| Richard M. Libenson | 35,000 | 332,014 | 338,408 | 705,422 |
| John W. Meisenbach | 35,000 | 332,014 | | 367,014 |
| Charles T. Munger | 45,000 | 332,014 | | 377,014 |
| Jeffrey S. Raikes | 38,000 | 332,014 | | 370,014 |
| Jill S. Ruckelshaus | 17,000 | 332,014 | | 349,014 |
| James D. Sinegal | 35,000 | 332,014 | | 367,014 |
| John W. Stanton[4] | 31,789 | 238,382 | | 270,171 |
| Mary Agnes (Maggie) Wilderotter | 34,982 | 332,014 | | 366,996 |

Executive compensation is one of the top reasons to read the proxy. The proxy will have a section wherein the board discusses (1) its compensation philosophy, (2) the role of the compensation committee, and (3) how executives are compensated.

**There are four main elements of any executive's**

**compensation.**

The first is a base salary, which is set at a competitive level relative to peers and competitors in the industry. Most companies will also award annual cash bonuses based on the achievement of financial targets.

These can vary significantly across various companies, but include some kind of revenue, profit, or cash flow metric.

Executives also receive equity (i.e. shares) as compensation. This can come in the form of options, restricted stock units, and performance-based restricted stock units.

*Stock options** represent the right to buy the company's stock at a predetermined price.

*Restricted stock units (RSUs)** are shares awarded to management that vest over multiple periods (most often over three to five years).

*Performance based restricted stock units** are RSUs that only vest if certain performance metrics have been achieved.

The management team may also receive a variety of other compensation benefits and perquisites such as corporate housing or a vehicle allowance. The level of these expenses vary on a company-by-company basis.

Management's compensation is summarized in a table near the end of the proxy in a table called "summary compensation table." This details management's compensation in each of the categories I mentioned over the past three years.

Here is Costco's summary compensation table from the latest proxy:

| Name and Principal Position | Year | Salary ($)[1] | Bonus ($)[2] | Stock Awards ($)[3] | Change in Pension Value and Nonqualified Deferred Compensation Earnings ($)[4] | All Other Compensation ($)[5] | Total ($) |
|---|---|---|---|---|---|---|---|
| W. Craig Jelinek | 2016 | 700,000 | 81,600 | 5,563,064 | 57,227 | 101,385 | 6,503,276 |
| President and Chief Executive Officer | 2015 | 698,079 | 188,800 | 5,322,962 | 35,319 | 95,233 | 6,340,393 |
| | 2014 | 651,731 | 90,400 | 4,783,200 | 8,541 | 90,786 | 5,624,658 |
| Jeffrey H. Brotman | 2016 | 650,000 | 81,600 | 5,563,064 | 78,842 | 108,248 | 6,481,754 |
| Chairman of the Board | 2015 | 650,000 | 188,800 | 5,322,962 | 45,513 | 103,303 | 6,310,578 |
| | 2014 | 650,000 | 90,400 | 4,783,200 | 10,735 | 95,517 | 5,629,852 |
| Richard A. Galanti | 2016 | 700,001 | 52,640 | 2,915,115 | 117,177 | 110,480 | 3,895,413 |
| Executive Vice President, Chief Financial Officer | 2015 | 699,041 | 75,520 | 2,794,440 | 74,173 | 102,583 | 3,745,757 |
| | 2014 | 683,654 | 36,160 | 2,511,180 | 17,859 | 103,915 | 3,352,768 |
| Dennis R. Zook | 2016 | 657,730 | 50,223 | 2,941,903 | 21,094 | 105,944 | 3,776,894 |
| Executive Vice President, COO- Southwest Division & Mexico | 2015 | 641,753 | 77,073 | 2,794,440 | 12,303 | 98,960 | 3,624,529 |
| | 2014 | 626,866 | 55,868 | 2,511,180 | 2,807 | 97,465 | 3,294,186 |
| Joseph P. Portera | 2016 | 660,231 | 52,039 | 2,915,115 | 26,549 | 115,718 | 3,769,652 |
| Executive Vice President, COO- Eastern & Canadian Divisions | 2015 | 644,431 | 78,259 | 2,794,440 | 18,093 | 110,286 | 3,645,509 |
| | 2014 | 629,713 | 56,047 | 2,511,180 | 5,465 | 108,032 | 3,310,437 |

# Form 4 Filings

Now that we've discussed the annual proxy statement, we can go over Form 4 filings.

All directors and officers must file documents with the SEC for changes in their share ownership. This provides more transparency to investors regarding the trading activities of people close with the Company.

**A Form 4s must be filed before the end of the second business day following a change in ownership (applies both stock sales and purchases).**

There is a lot of information contained in Form 4s. All form 4s have transaction codes detailing the nature of why the filing was needed.

Here are some of the most common:

If there is a **P code,** it means the person bought shares in the open market or purchased shares in a private transaction.

A **S code** means the person sold shares in the open market or sold it to someone else in a private transaction.

An **A code** is used with the insider received a grant, award, or otherwise acquired shares from the Company itself.

A **D code** means the person sold or transferred shares back to the Company.

A **F code** means the shares were withheld or sold to pay for the exercise price of options or to settle a tax liability for shares received from the Company.

A **M code** is used when the insider exercises or converts a security received from the Company. For example, if the insider exercised options, that would require a M code.

When an insider gifts shares to someone else or another entity, it is reported under a **G code**. Now, this can because they gifted the shares to a family member or if they donated the shares to charity.

Before we move on to the next section, let's just briefly discuss a few questions we need to ask ourselves as analysts when looking over form 4s.

First, we need to consider how many insiders are buying shares or selling shares. Obviously, if more than one insider is selling shares, it increases the likelihood that they may not think too favorably of the Company's prospects.

Let's take a look at one of Costco's recent Form 4 filings. Here's one from December 2016:

The first section of the Form 4 gives details on who is filing the document. In this case it is Timothy Rose, an Executive Vice President.

| SEC Form 4 | | | |
|---|---|---|---|
| **FORM 4** | **UNITED STATES SECURITIES AND EXCHANGE COMMISSION** Washington, D.C. 20549 | | **OMB APPROVAL** |
| | | | OMB Number: 3235-0287 |
| Check this box if no longer subject to Section 16. Form 4 or Form 5 obligations may continue. See Instruction 1(b). | **STATEMENT OF CHANGES IN BENEFICIAL OWNERSHIP** | | Estimated average burden hours per response: 0.5 |
| | Filed pursuant to Section 16(a) of the Securities Exchange Act of 1934 or Section 30(h) of the Investment Company Act of 1940 | | |
| 1. Name and Address of Reporting Person* Rose Timothy L. | 2. Issuer Name **and** Ticker or Trading Symbol COSTCO WHOLESALE CORP /NEW [ COST ] | 5. Relationship of Reporting Person(s) to Issuer (Check all applicable) Director / 10% Owner / X Officer (give title below) / Other (specify below) Executive VP | |
| (Last) (First) (Middle) 999 LAKE DRIVE | 3. Date of Earliest Transaction (Month/Day/Year) 03/16/2017 | | |
| (Street) ISSAQUAH WA 98027 | 4. If Amendment, Date of Original Filed (Month/Day/Year) | 6. Individual or Joint/Group Filing (Check Applicable Line) X Form filed by One Reporting Person / Form filed by More than One Reporting Person | |
| (City) (State) (Zip) | | | |

The second part of the Form 4 is a table detailing the transaction(s) that occurred. For instance, we can see here that the transaction occurred on 03/16/17. Timothy Rose sold shares given the "S" transaction code. He sold 4,000 shares at $166.95

per-share.

| Table I - Non-Derivative Securities Acquired, Disposed of, or Beneficially Owned | | | | | | | | | |
|---|---|---|---|---|---|---|---|---|---|
| 1. Title of Security (Instr. 3) | 2. Transaction Date (Month/Day/Year) | 2A. Deemed Execution Date, if any (Month/Day/Year) | 3. Transaction Code (Instr. 8) | | 4. Securities Acquired (A) or Disposed Of (D) (Instr. 3, 4 and 5) | | | 5. Amount of Securities Beneficially Owned Following Reported Transaction(s) (Instr. 3 and 4) | 6. Ownership Form: Direct (D) or Indirect (I) (Instr. 4) | 7. Nature of Indirect Beneficial Ownership (Instr. 4) |
| | | | Code | V | Amount | (A) or (D) | Price | | | |
| Common Stock | 03/16/2017 | | S | | 4,000 | D | $166.9498[1] | 44,049 | D | |

| Table II - Derivative Securities Acquired, Disposed of, or Beneficially Owned (e.g., puts, calls, warrants, options, convertible securities) | | | | | | | | | | |
|---|---|---|---|---|---|---|---|---|---|---|
| 1. Title of Derivative Security (Instr. 3) | 2. Conversion or Exercise Price of Derivative Security | 3. Transaction Date (Month/Day/Year) | 3A. Deemed Execution Date, if any (Month/Day/Year) | 4. Transaction Code (Instr. 8) | 5. Number of Derivative Securities Acquired (A) or Disposed of (D) (Instr. 3, 4 and 5) | 6. Date Exercisable and Expiration Date (Month/Day/Year) | 7. Title and Amount of Securities Underlying Derivative Security (Instr. 3 and 4) | 8. Price of Derivative Security (Instr. 5) | 9. Number of derivative Securities Beneficially Owned Following Reported Transaction(s) (Instr. 4) | 10. Ownership Form: Direct (D) or Indirect (I) (Instr. 4) | 11. Nature of Indirect Beneficial Ownership (Instr. 4) |
| | | | | Code | V | (A) | (D) | Date Exercisable | Expiration Date | Title | Amount or Number of Shares | | | | |

Explanation of Responses:

1. The price shown is a weighted average sale price for shares sold in multiple transactions; the sale prices ranged from $166.90 to $167.02 per share. The reporting person will provide to the issuer, any security holder of the issuer, or the SEC staff, upon request, information regarding the number of shares sold at each price within the range.

As you can see, a wealth of information can be gleamed from these Form 4 filings. That's why it's so important to read every single one.

When reading over Form 4s, we need to consider if any of the share purchases or sales were significant.

We do this by comparing the purchase or sale relative to the beneficial ownership disclosed in the proxy statement. Generally speaking, if the purchase or sale represented more than a 10% movement in beneficial ownership, I consider it to be important.

**Quarterly Results**

Public companies in the U.S. are required to report results on a quarterly basis. Companies will typically set reporting dates for these results 2 or 3 weeks in advance.

Keep an eye out for the 8-K or press release detailing the financial results.

**Quarterly results will be announced in an 8-K prior to the release of the 10-Q or 10-K.** This is because the 10-Q and 10-K are larger filings and require more work to complete.

The disclosure in the quarterly results will differ on a company-by-company basis, however I have listed out some of the key elements below.

The first part will include a quick recap of the quarter and some financial highlights. This may be followed up with management commentary or a quote from the management team.

If the company provides financial guidance, it will most likely be released in the quarterly results.

The quarterly results include abbreviated financial statements (although some companies do disclose full financial statements).

Finally, if the company reports any non-GAAP metrics, these will be disclosed near the end of the quarterly results report.

The quarterly results announcement can significantly impact the stock price. Many analysts cover stocks and publish estimates for various sales and earnings metrics.

**Stocks react (i.e. move) in response to these earnings surprises. If the company beats or reports results higher than analyst expectations, it is called a positive surprise.**

If the results are below analyst expectations, it is called a negative surprise.

**Financial Guidance**

Earlier we briefly touched on financial guidance. Companies can provide guidance for the next quarter or even for the current fiscal year on a variety of metrics including revenue, margins, profit, store openings, capital expenditures, and more.

Guidance is not required by SEC reporting standards and is entirely voluntary. Like earnings results, it is important to pay attention to the guidance surprise.

**If the company provides financial guidance above analyst expectations, the stock may react favorably.** Conversely, if guidance is below expectations, the stock may decline.

**Non-GAAP Metrics**

In the U.S. companies report under generally accepted accounting principles or U.S. GAAP.

**Some companies also report non-GAAP metrics in their quarterly results to provide additional insight into the results.** These non-GAAP results adjust for items the company believes are one-time or do not reflect the earnings power of the business.

Common adjustments under non-GAAP metrics include:

**\*Stock-based compensation:** This is more prevalent for companies in the technology industry where stock comp can be a very large expense.

**\*Restructuring and impairment charges**: Some companies adjust for restructuring and impairment charges because these are "one time" items taken to improve results.

**\*EBITDA**: Many companies in the mining and construction industry report a metric called earnings before interest, taxes, depreciation, and amortization (also known as EBITDA).

**\*Acquisition-related expenses**: If the company makes acquisitions, expenses related to that are typically excluded. These expenses may include costs for lawyers, advisors, and other third-party services.

If a company reports non-GAAP results, they must provide a reconciliation to the related GAAP metric.

As analysts, we must determine if a company's non-GAAP metrics is appropriate. **Sometimes management's use of adjustments in non-GAAP results can be aggressive**. In fact, the use of non-GAAP metrics is a highly controversial topic in the accounting world.

Some believe that non-GAAP metrics allow companies to bypass U.S. GAAP and report whatever they want, which can mislead investors to the health and performance of the business.

Proponents of non-GAAP metrics say that it allows investors to disregard certain one-time, non-recurring, or extraordinary items because they do not reflect the core earnings and cash flow generation capability of the business.

**Conference Calls**

Conference calls are used by nearly all public companies to report quarterly results. Conference calls are typically scheduled a few weeks in advance via a press release.

Many conference calls are also accompanied by presentation slides, which can be accessed on the company's investor relations website.

These presentation slides make it easier to follow along on the call. **They sometimes provide additional details or information that may not be included in the earnings releases or other SEC filings.**

Most conference calls are very structured and follow three phases.

*First, the call always begins with a disclaimer wherein the company cites certain legal language that management may express opinions and guidance that are subjective. It's basically a disclaimer to cover their legal bases. This portion of the call is usually two to three minutes long.

*Next, the management team will comment on the results of the quarter, any notable highlights, or even financial guidance. This part of the call can last anywhere between five minutes and half an hour.

*After management's prepared remarks, the Company will conduct a live Q&A session with analysts. This part of the call can easily last over 30 minutes depending on how many questions are asked.

The audio of the quarterly conference call is usually kept on the company's investor relations website for a limited time. Quarterly conference call transcripts are available from a number of websites for free, including Seeking Alpha.

**Reading through conference call transcripts and listening to the audio is a great way to learn more about the company because you might get additional information that is not disclosed in the financials or anywhere else.**

Further, if you listen to the audio, you can get a sense of management's tone of voice.

## Key performance Indicators (KPIs)

To be a successful financial analyst, you need to be able to identify and track a company's key performance indicators also known as KPIs.

KPIs are typically disclosed and discussed in earnings releases, conference calls, and the MD&A section of SEC filings.

Some industries have very specific KPIs that are widely used. We'll walk through the most popular ones.

## Same Store Sales

Let's start off with same store sales, which is sometimes referred to comparable sales or comp sales or simply just 'comps'.

Before defining same store sales, let's go through an example to see why it is a useful metric.

Say we decided to start a retail company in year 1 and generated $100 of sales. In year 2, that same store generated $90 of sales. During year 2, we also opened a second store which generated an additional $100 in sales. As a result, our total year 2 sales across both stores is $190.

On the surface, it looks like our year 2 sales increased 90%! However, looking more closely, the only reason why sales increased was because we opened a second store. Our original store actually experienced a 10% decline in sales!

That's why same store sales can be a very useful metric. **Same store sales attempts to compare sales from existing outlets in both years for a like-for-like comparison.** We want to compare sales of stores that were open during both the current year and the prior year.

So in the prior example, same store sales would be negative 10% growth.

Same store sales is a widely used metric by retail companies and restaurants.

**Keep in mind that not all companies have the same definition of same store sales.**

Some companies may only calculate same store sales for

stores that were open in both periods. Some calculate it based on stores that have been open for at least 2 years. Always read the disclosures on how the metric is calculated.

**Organic Growth**

Sometimes companies acquire other businesses for strategic purposes or to expand into new markets. The question then becomes how do we calculate a comparable revenue metric to evaluate performance?

Let's go through another example to see why organic growth is an important metric.

Say Company A is growing revenue at 5% a year, while Company B is growing at 15% a year...which one sounds like a better investment?

It sounds like Company B, because it's growing faster. Well...what if Company B is not actually growing. In fact, what if the 15% growth is entirely because it acquired other businesses! In other words, the "organic" core business is not increasing! You'd probably look at the business much differently, right?

That is what organic growth measures. **Organic growth measures revenue growth through a company's own business activities such as price increases, volume increases, or new products.**

<u>This is in contrast to inorganic growth refers to revenue growth arising from mergers and acquisitions.</u>

When evaluating the growth of a company, it is important to consider how much of growth is organic and how much is inorganic.

**Constant Currency**

Some companies have major foreign operations which expose them to currency risk. Let's go through an example to see how foreign currency can play out.

Let's say we are a U.S. based manufacturer and sell our goods to the U.K. in pounds.

In year 1, we generate £100 in sales. If the exchange rate is 1 British pound per US dollar, our sales for year 1 would simply be $100.

In year 2, let's say we generated another £100 in sales. However, the exchange rate is now 1 British pound per $1.3 US dollars. In other words, the dollar is weaker! When we translate our pounds back to US dollars, we will have $130 in sales.

Just looking at our dollar-based sales, it would appear that business is great! However, our sales in British pounds were flat year-over-year.

This is when the use of constant currency comes in handy. **Constant currency eliminates the impact of exchange rates on financial results.** We can use constant currency to compare revenue, expenses, margins, and many more metrics.

Constant currency is most useful with companies that have significant international operations.

Going back to our example, our constant currency revenue growth would be 0%, because we generate £100 in sales in both years.

**Bookings & Backlog**

Bookings and backlog are both non-GAAP metrics typically used by engineering/construction firms, certain manufacturers, and industrial companies.

Bookings, which can also be referred to as orders, represent the dollar value of contracts awarded during the period. It does not necessarily represent the amount of revenue that will be recognized because contracts can be canceled or modified. Bookings is utilized to assess business volume and revenue trajectory.

Backlog is a similar metric to bookings. Backlog refers to the buildup of work that needs to be completed--in other words, it refers to orders or bookings that still need to be finished.

**Bookings and backlog are utilized by analysts to assess business volume and a company's potential short-term revenue potential.**

As I mentioned before, financial statement analysis is the backbone of successful investing.

Most investors are too lazy (or don't know how) to really dig through SEC filings. With this knowledge, you can get a real competitive edge on other investors.

Thank you for reading and I hope this book was helpful!

If you enjoyed this book, please consider leaving a review!

**P.S.** Check out the next page to get a great deal on my amazing financial statements analysis online course!

If you'd like to learn more about financial statement analysis, click here (https://goo.gl/uNZdgE) to get a great deal on my financial statement video course. **It contains over 3 hours of amazing content.**

The video lectures cover many of the topics discussed in this book, but in more detail. Plus, it includes several case study examples and detailed walk throughs of SEC filings.

It took me years of self-learning and on-the-job experience to learn all of this. And now you get to benefit from my struggles!

This course will be available to loyal book readers for **only $35 (normally $150+)!**

**PLUS I'm giving away a ton of FREE BONUS CONTENT in this course, including:**

● **Video guide (the SEC Edgar database):** Learn how to navigate through the SEC Edgar database like a pro! **($25+ VALUE)**

● **Video guide (Form 4 filings):** Learn how to pull up insider filings to see executive stock purchases and sales! **($15+ VALUE)**

- **How to use Google Finance**: How to read stock charts on Google Finance and navigate the website! **($20+ VALUE)**

- **How to use investor relations**: How to use investor relations to pull important information **($20+ VALUE)**

- **Video guide (SEC Letters)**: How to use public SEC Letters to get a real competitive advantage. **($30+ VALUE)**

- **Financial ratios cheat sheet**: Learn how to use over 15 important financial metrics and ratios to analyze stocks **($50+ VALUE)**!

<u>That's right! You're getting EXTRA content valued at $160+ for FREE!</u>

Don't miss out on this opportunity. The quality of the content isn't even available in most $60,000+ MBA schools!

**<u>Click here</u> and learn how to analyze financial statements like a pro!**

71905883R00066

Made in the USA
San Bernardino, CA
20 March 2018